Animal Spikes and Spines

Rebecca Rissman

www.heinemannraintree.com
Visit our website to find out more information about Heinemann-Raintree books.

To order:

☎ Phone 888-454-2279

🖱 Visit www.heinemannraintree.com to browse our catalog and order online.

Edited by Rebecca Rissman, Daniel Nunn, and Harriet Milles
Designed by Joanna Hinton-Malivoire
Picture research by Tracy Cummins
Originated by Capstone Global Library Ltd.
Production by Victoria Fitzgerald
Printed and bound in China by Leo Paper Products Ltd

15 14 13 12 11
10 9 8 7 6 5 4 3 2 1

Library of Congress Cataloging-in-Publication Data
Rissman, Rebecca.
  Animal Spikes and Spines / Rebecca Rissman.
      p. cm.
  Includes bibliographical references and index.
  ISBN 978-1-4329-5355-3 (hc)—ISBN 978-1-4329-5500-7 (pb) 1.
Anatomy, Comparative—Juvenile literature. I. Title.
  QL806.5.R573 2012
  591.4—dc22 2010044799

Acknowledgments
The author and publishers are grateful to the following for permission to reproduce copyright material: iStockphoto **pp. 7** (© Brandon Alms), **9** (© Ken Canning), **15** (© Craig Dingle), **21 left** (© Tom Tietz), **21 right** (© beltsazar); Minden **p. 17** (© Donald M. Jones); National Geographic Stock **p. 20 right** (© PAUL NICKLEN); Shutterstock **pp. 4** (© Utekhina Anna), **5 left** (© Hiroshi Sato), **5 right** (© irin-k), **10, 22c** (© Ronnie Howard), **11, 22a** (© Nick Biemans), **12** (© ecoventurestravel), **13** (© Maria Dryfhout), **14** (© FloridaStock), **16, 22f** (© MartinMaritz), **18, 22d** (© Hazeelin Hassan), **19, 22e** (© Francois Etienne du Plessis), **20 left** (© Undersea Discoveries), **22b** (© Four Oaks).

Cover photographs reproduced with permission of iStockphoto (© Grafissimo and © Paul Tessier), Photolibrary, and Shutterstock (©H. Damke and © Kate Connes). Back cover photo reproduced with permission of Shutterstock (© MartinMaritz).

We would like to thank Michael Bright for his invaluable help in the preparation of this book.

Every effort has been made to contact copyright holders of any material reproduced in this book. Any omissions will be rectified in subsequent printings if notice is given to the publisher.

Some words appear in bold, **like this.** You can find out what they mean in "Words to Know" on page 23.

Contents

About this series

Books in this series introduce readers to different animals' spiky or spiny body parts. Use this book to stimulate discussion about why animals have these body parts and how they use them.

Animal Body Parts

ear

tail

feet

leg

Animals have different body parts. Some body parts help animals get around. Body parts such as legs and feet help animals run. Body parts such as flippers and fins help animals to swim.

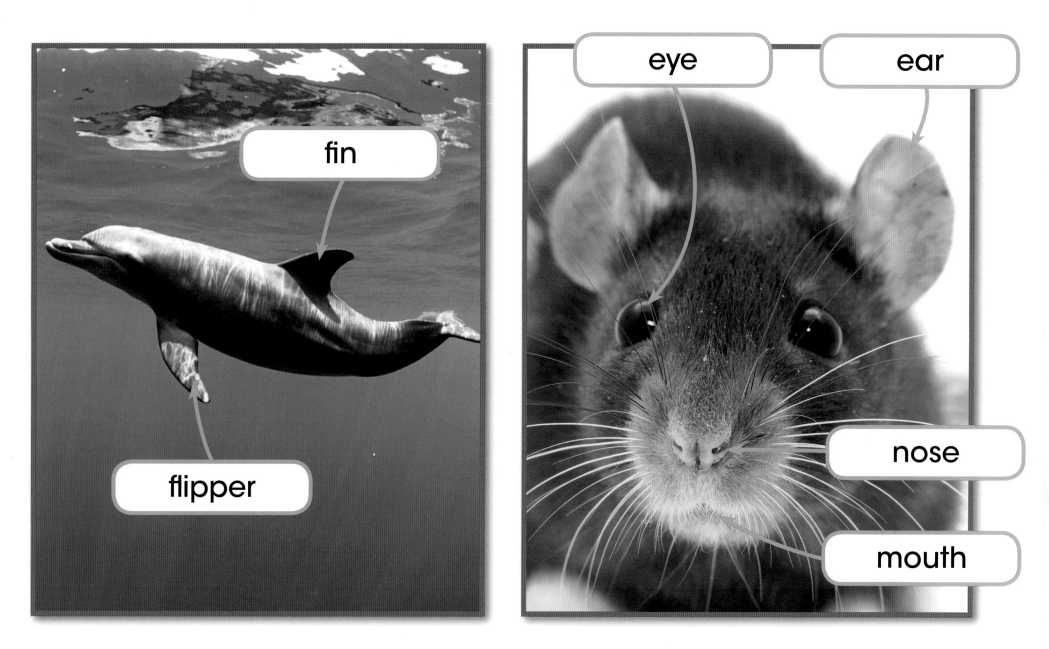

fin

flipper

eye

ear

nose

mouth

Some body parts help animals **sense** the world.
Animals use their eyes to see. Animals use their
ears to hear. Animals use their noses to smell.
Animals use their mouths to taste.

5

Why Do Animals Have Different Body Parts?

giraffe

Animals have different body parts to help them survive. Animals live in different **habitats**. Animals have body parts that help them to live in their habitat.

frog

Some animals are **predators**, or hunters. Their
body parts help them to catch **prey** to eat. Some
animals are prey. Other animals hunt them. Their
body parts help them to stay safe.

Ready to Fight

antelope

horns

Some body parts help animals to fight. Some animals use **horns** to fight. Horns grow from animals' heads. Antelope use their horns to fight other antelope.

beak

heron

Some animals use **beaks** to fight. Beaks grow on birds' heads. Beaks can be sharp. Beaks can be strong. Herons uses their beaks to peck at other herons and other animals.

antlers

moose

Some animals use **antlers** to fight. Antlers grow from animals' heads. Antlers are very hard. Moose sometimes use their antlers to fight other moose to see who is stronger.

tiger

claws

Some animals use **claws** to fight. Claws grow on animals' feet. Claws can be very sharp. Tigers use their claws to fight other tigers and other animals.

Ready to Hunt

cayman

teeth

Some body parts help animals hunt. Animals hunt in order to catch and eat other animals. Some animals' teeth can be very sharp. Cayman catch **prey** with their sharp teeth.

snake

fangs

venom

Some animals' teeth are very long. Some snakes
have long teeth called **fangs**. They use their fangs
to catch prey. They bite other animals and put
venom into their bodies. Then they eat them!

eagle

talons

Some animals use **claws** to catch **prey**. Claws can be very long. Eagles have long claws called **talons**. Eagles use their talons to snatch animals off the ground. They can snatch fish out of water, too.

beak

pelican

Some animals use **beaks** to catch prey. Beaks can be very long. Beaks can be very wide. Pelicans can use their beaks to catch fish. They scoop up the fish in their big beaks.

Ready to Scare

spines

porcupine

Some body parts help scare other animals away. Some animals use **spines** to scare other animals away. Spines can be long. Porcupines use their spines to scare other animals away.

wolf

antlers

elk

Some animals use **antlers** to scare other animals away. Elk use their antlers to scare away **predators**, such as wolves.

beak

raven

Some birds use sounds to scare away other animals.
This raven opens its **beak** to let out a loud warning.
It tells other birds and animals to stay away.

baboon

teeth

Some animals show their teeth to scare other animals away. This baboon shows its long, sharp teeth to warn other animals to stay away.

Finding Spikes and Spines

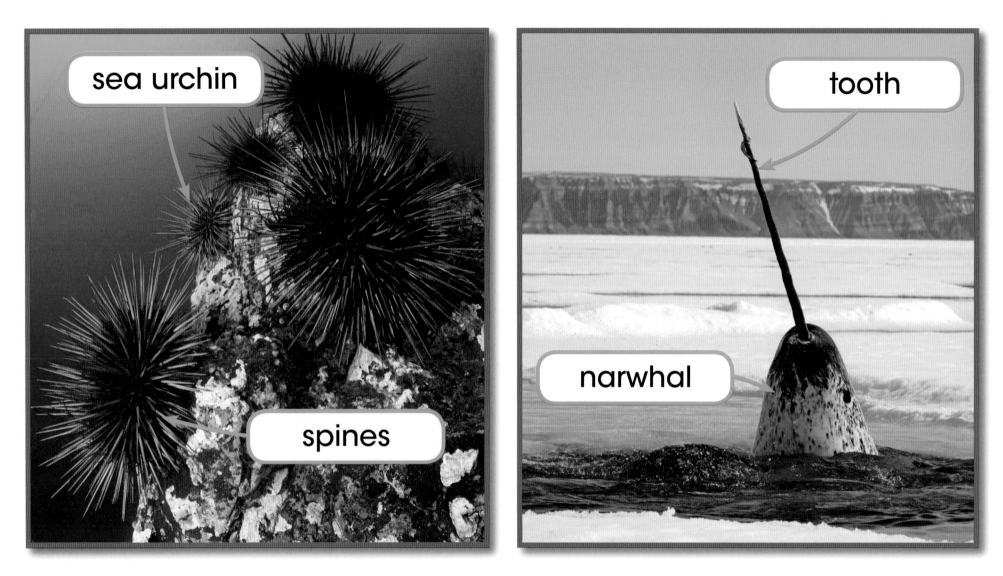

sea urchin

spines

tooth

narwhal

Animals all over Earth have spikes and **spines**. Sea urchins live in the ocean. They use spines to keep fish away. Narwhals live in the ocean near the North Pole. They use a long tooth to fight other narwhals.

horn

parrot

lizard

beak

Horned lizards live in the desert. They use their **horns** to scare other animals away. Parrots live in forests. They can use their **beaks** to fight with other birds.

Animal Body Parts Close Up

Can you remember what all these animal body parts are called?

Answers on page 24

Words to Know

antler hard body part that grows on the head of an animal, such as a moose

beak hard, pointed part of a bird's mouth

claw long, pointed nails that grow on some animals' paws or feet

fang long, sharp tooth of a fierce animal

habitat place where an animal lives, or a plant grows

horn hard, pointed object that grows out of some animals' heads

predator animal that hunts and eats other animals

prey animal that is hunted and eaten by other animals

sense ways that animals understand the world around them. Seeing, smelling, hearing, tasting, and feeling are senses.

spine stiff spike that grows on some animals, such as porcupines

talon long, hooked claw on the foot of a large bird

Index

Answers to quiz on page 22:
a) claws b) horns c) antlers d) beak e) teeth f) spines

Note to Parents and Teachers

Before reading

Show the children the front cover of the book. Guide children in a discussion about what they think the book will be about. Tell children that animals have different body parts that are used for different things.

After reading

- Pass around some pictures of animals with different body parts. Tell the children to go back to their seats with a partner and sort their animals into different body part groups. For example, animals with sharp teeth, animals with tails, and animals with spikes. Then ask the children about particular animals. For instance: "Does a tiger have a beak?" (No); "Does an antelope have horns?" (Yes).